Leading The Pack

By

Nick Russell

Contents

Introduction

Since the inception of business, organizations have searched for clues to help identify and select successful leaders. They have searched for men and women of vision with that rare combination of traits that help them serve as motivator, business driver, and authority figure. The concept of leadership has been widely observed and frequently studied, but a thorough understanding of what defines successful leadership has always remained just out of reach.

There was an interest in finding the answer(s) to the age-old question, "What makes a great leader?" After studying the behavioral attributes of thousands of business leaders, the resulting data could reveal commonalities that define strong leadership. What similar patterns or behaviors might possibly be found over and over again? By forming a concise "leadership recipe," the never-ending search for quality leaders could finally be simplified to a standardized set of characteristics that might help predict successful leadership in any organization. But could science and behavioral psychology be successfully applied to extract these leadership "revelations" from the data?

The investigation was centered on behavioral leadership models that were used across 24 unique companies encompassing 4,512 business leaders from all performance levels. These companies included several from the Fortune 500 list. Each of the 30 leadership models was analyzed to identify the most common behaviors that differentiate higher-performing leaders from low-performing leaders. The findings compiled from this data set revealed new evidence that must serve as a foundational piece of every leadership hiring or training endeavor.

Leadership is a concept that is difficult to capture. You know it when you see it, but it is difficult to quantify. The components of leadership are often examined and observed, but the ability to predict successful leadership has thus far avoided the confines of a repeatable recipe. Many approaches have been used in an attempt to document commonalities among successful leaders, but only with mixed results at best. Taking a new approach to the issue, I set out to study the behavioral characteristics of successful leaders in comparison to leaders of lower performance levels. The two main objectives of this study were:

To identify the three most important behaviors that are predictive of leadership performance.

To identify the level or degree of the three most common behaviors that are predictive of leadership performance.

Behavioral Leadership Models

Before discussing the study findings, it is important to lay the groundwork of this study using the behavioral leadership model. The behavioral leadership model is the cornerstone to this research study since it is designed to capture the behavioral preferences of successful leaders currently working in the position. Essentially, the behavioral leadership model captures the unique combination of behaviors that predicts success. Each unique model was created using the same methodology, but the customization was made possible by using performance data related to a specific position. To create a behavioral leadership model, each organization used the following three-step process.

Define Success-Traditionally, leadership success is determined by education, experience, potential, or other non-performance related measures. For this study, success was determined by actual performance on the job. We want to better understand the behaviors of the real leaders who produce results on a daily basis.

To keep the study focused on leadership productivity, each company defined success based on their business practices, and their leaders were evaluated on their ability to produce the desired business results. Those who did not produce the desired outcomes were considered ineffective leaders while others who produced the desired results were considered successful leaders. Each organization utilized specific performance data captured from those leaders actively engaged in the leadership role. The types of performance data collected ranged from subjective data (i.e., performance evaluations, soft achievement ratings, etc.) to objective data (i.e., store sales, percent to plan, profit metrics, etc.).

Use a Behavioral Assessment-The objective in this step is to capture the behavioral preferences of each leader (across all levels of success). The leaders in each organization were assessed using a behavioral assessment tool that measured 38 core behaviors. The 38 behaviors provided insight into the deeper motivations and preferences of each leader.

Build a Leadership Model-To create the leadership model, the behavioral assessment data was combined with the performance data for each leadership role. The result was a behavioral depiction of successful leadership across 38 behaviors. The leadership model determined how important each dimension was when compared to all 38 behaviors. Understanding the importance provides insight into the comparative ability of each behavior in predicting leadership performance. Equally as important is the degree in which the dimension needs to exist (ex: "high" Attention to Detail, "medium" Assertiveness, or "low" Insight into Others). The degree of a behavior will greatly affect leadership in terms of productivity, communication, and many other leadership activities.

.

Each leadership model was constructed in the same manner. The specific combination of dimensions (both importance and degree) was a reflection of current performance data from active leaders in the role. The models were customized to capture the true essence of leadership as it exists on the job and as it relates specifically to daily performance or contribution to the organization.

Behavioral Leadership Study

For this study, leadership roles were analyzed across 30 leadership models using the behavioral and performance data of 4,512 business leaders. For each role, a unique leadership model was created to assemble the strongest predictors of leadership according to behavioral preferences as they relate to actual quantified performance on the job. The process included comparing each of the 30 leadership models in a search for common behaviors predictive of leadership success (also considering the importance and degree). The study was based on the following parameters:

There were (n = 24) companies represented, some with multi-billion-dollar annual revenues, across (n = 10) industries: Medical, Grocery, Retail, Financial, Restaurant, Hotel, Food Service, Property Management, Industrial, and Customer Service.

Successful leadership was defined as a consistent and quantified achievement of current business objectives as designated by the organization. For example, in situations where the organization defined leadership success as achieving a higher "percent to plan," good performance was reflected through a consistent and strong production of high "percent to plan" numbers.

The average tenure for the (n = 4,512) leaders with varying performance levels was 2,242 days (over six years).

For descriptive purposes, leadership roles were banded according to range of responsibility. For this study sample, Level 1 leaders, or 36.67%, are responsible for a small direct group of employees. Level 2, or 56.67% of the sample, are responsible for a location, site, store, or entire office. Level 3, or 6.67%, were responsible for a region, multiple sites, multiple stores, multiple locations, or multiple offices.

Importance-Most Frequently Occurring Behaviors

Over the course of the study, each of the 30 leadership models was analyzed and the top ten "most predictive" behaviors were recorded and compared. The objective was to use the top ten behaviors across the 30 models as the method to capture the most predictive behaviors.

The next step was to identify the three most common behaviors (out of the top ten) across the 30 leadership models. The focus was limited to the top three most common behaviors to provide a more concise view of successful leadership. By identifying the three most frequently occurring behaviors, insights would be gained into the three most important behaviors that predict leadership success across a wide variety of leadership roles in a wide variety of industries. The data showed some surprising results:

Interestingly, all 38 behavioral dimensions were represented somewhere within the lists of top ten behaviors across the 30 leadership models.

Least Important Behaviors-There were two behaviors that were consistently the lowest in importance. Reflective (deep thinking and/or the ability to anticipate long-term outcomes) and Team Orientation (desire to work with groups) had the lowest frequency, occurring in just 10.00% of the models.

Most Important Behavior-Across all 30 of the leadership models, Energy appeared in the top ten more than any other behavior (14 out of 30, or 46.67%) among all the leadership models. The mere presence of Energy in the behavioral model did not indicate the degree most suitable for the position, only that it played an important role in the overall behavioral evaluation for successful leadership.

Second-Most Important Behavior-The dimension of Competitive Fierceness appeared in 13 out of 30, or 43.33%, of the top ten lists of the leadership models studied. Some successful leaders may be more competitive while others prefer a supportive environment. As with Energy, Competitive Fierceness was found to be a primary part of many behavioral models in varying degrees.

Third-Most Important Behavior-Acceptance of Authority appeared in 12 out of 30, or 40.00%, of the top ten lists of the leadership models studied. Whether these 12 behavioral models required a high, medium, or low degree of this dimension required further study (see the following section).

There were 38 behavioral characteristics studied across the 30 leadership models. The objective was to find the most predictive or most frequently occurring behaviors that drive successful leadership. The research data revealed that Energy, Competitive Fierceness, and Acceptance of Authority appeared in the top ten lists most frequently. The most predictive or most frequently occurring behaviors provide the avenue to further explore the degree or amount of each behavior needed to predict leadership success for each of these three behaviors.

Challenging Leadership Assumptions

Based on the three most important or predictive leadership behaviors (Energy, Competitive Fierceness, and Acceptance of Authority), assumptions can be formed based on common (natural) perceptions of successful leadership. It is a common practice to assume that successful leaders exhibit a strong relation to, or very high degree of, a particular behavior. For the purpose of this study, I examined the varying degrees required to be successful across each of these three important behaviors.

Assumption #1 - Leaders must be "high energy" to be successful.

Energy was considered the most predictive (or most frequently occurring) behavior in 14 of 30, or 46.67%, of the leadership models.

• 21% of the models required below average Energy levels

• 37% of the models required average Energy levels

• 21% of the models required an above average Energy level

• 21% of the models required high Energy levels

• 0% of the models required an extremely high level of Energy

Although the majority of the leadership models required an above average amount of Energy, there were no models that required extraordinary levels of Energy.

Assumption #2 - Successful leaders must be highly competitive to be successful.

Competitive Fierceness was a top ten behavior in 13 of 30, or 43.33%, of the leadership models studied.

• 23% of the models required a more Supportive approach

• 39% of the models required a balance between being supportive and competitive

• 38% of the models required a more competitive approach

• 0% of the models required a high level of Competitive Fierceness

• 0% of the models required an extremely high level of Competitive Fierceness

The majority of the leadership models required an average to slightly above average level of Competitive Fierceness. None of the leadership models required a high or extremely high level of Competitive Fierceness.

Assumption #3 - Successful leaders need a more rebellious nature to be a high performer.

According to the data studied, Acceptance of Authority was considered one of the most predictive behaviors in 12 of 30, or 40.00%, of the leadership models.

• 42% of the models required a more rebellious approach

• 41% of the models required a balance between accepting authority and being rebellious

• 17% of the models required a more Acceptance of Authority approach

• 0% of the models required a high level of Acceptance of Authority

• 0% of the models required an extremely high level of Acceptance of Authority

According to the data studied, 84% of the leadership models required a below average or average level of Acceptance of Authority. None of the leadership models required a high or extremely high level of Acceptance of Authority.

Conclusions Drawn from the Study

Data Point #1-All 38 behaviors play a role in successful leadership. It is important to point out that across the leadership models studied, all 38 behaviors appeared in the top ten of at least two or more of the leadership models. The entire group of 38 behaviors was present and accounted for in identifying successful leadership. This helps us to better understand the need to view each behavior as potentially valuable.

Conclusion-there were no behaviors that could be ignored or excluded from the recipe for successful leadership.

Data Point #2-Successful leadership behaviors are situational. Even the most common or frequently occurring leadership behavior showed up in less than 50% of the models. Stated another way, slightly more than half of the 30 leadership models did not consider Energy (the most frequently occurring behavior) as an important differentiator in identifying successful leadership. The data does not support the notion of a universal or "off-the-shelf" behavioral leadership model that will predict successful leadership.

Conclusion-there was no cut-and-dried combination of behaviors that predicted successful leadership (not even some of the time).

Data Point #3-Most leadership roles required higher than average levels of Energy, but not as high as you might think. Only 21% of the leadership models required high levels of Energy and none of the leadership models required extremely high levels of Energy.

By definition, a high level of Energy is often manifested through lots of activity, but the negative byproduct is hyperactivity, waste, and inefficiency. Practically, an above average level of Energy translates to the leader's ability to keep a group of people focused and moving at the proper pace and in the proper direction without the frustration of hyperactivity. From the follower's perspective, it is important to understand the implications of a sporadic or over-reactive leadership style (extremely high Energy). Think of how frustrating it is to do something and then redo it "just to stay busy" or doing busy work just "because the boss can't sit still." Associates perceive this style as scattered, confusing, and they struggle to find success and fulfillment under such a leadership style. Over time, credibility and respect can be lost, leaving this type of leader ineffective.

Conclusion-The most successful leaders possess above average amounts of energy, but not too much!

Data Point #4-Great leaders are competitive, but they also understand the importance of being supportive. According to the data, 23% of the leadership models required a more supportive approach to leading others. Combined with the 39% of leadership models that required a balanced approach, these findings provide helpful insights to the task of understanding strong leadership. Intuitively, the concept of balancing support with competition makes leadership sense. Leaders must know when competition is appropriate and when being supportive of those around them is more valuable than competing. Think of it as healthy competition-knowing when to turn the competitive juices on and when to turn them off. Without a firm grasp of this concept, overly competitive leaders may alienate those around them and create toxic environments.

Conclusion-A balance of respect for authority and rebelliousness is a common predictor of successful leadership.

Data Point #5-This we know to be true: successful leaders tend to challenge conventional structure and rules. In fact, 42% of the leadership models required a more rebellious approach to leadership. Many organizations rely on their leaders to challenge the current structure and methods that have been historically successful (or unsuccessful, as the case may be). Strong leaders often have an eye for creating positive change that removes stumbling blocks to success.

However, do not go overboard and think that your next leadership hire must behave like James Dean in "Rebel Without a Cause." Keep in mind that 41% of the leadership models required a balance between following authority and challenging the establishment. Not to be forgotten, another 17% of the leadership models required leaders to accept and embrace the structure around them. The practical reality is that successful leaders know how to "choose their battles." Sometimes being a rebel is productive and provides the necessary change, but that must be balanced with the recognition of situations where one must accept the current structure and operate within it.

Defining Leadership

Here are 3 popular ways of defining leadership, each from a slightly different perspective:

Leadership means being the dominant individual in a group.

Leadership means getting things done through people.

Leadership means challenging the status quo, promoting a better way.

For many, leadership means doing all three of these things but there are subtle and important differences. Let's look at them one by one.

Leadership means being the dominant individual in a group.

In primitive tribes and higher animal species the dominant individual was the leader. Being the leader simply meant having the power to attain and hold the top position for a reasonable length of time. Contrary to definition 2, you could be the leader without getting anything done through others. A leader was the person in charge even if the group was in a stable state where people went about their business as normal. As long as group members obeyed the leader's rules, the leader did not even need to be actively involved in the lives of group members, let alone get anything done through them. You could also be the leader in such a group without promoting a better way as suggested by definition 3. If you didn't need to be voted into power, why have a platform for change? You simply seized power; no sales pitch was needed on how you could make life better for the group. Yes, such leaders may have led groups successfully in battle and built great monuments with them, but, strictly speaking, you could be the leader without achieving anything through a group effort. The meaning of leadership, according to this definition, is simply to be at the top of the pile.

Leadership means getting things done through people.

Great leaders throughout history have led their groups to momentous achievements, but the idea that leadership should be defined as getting things done through people has been developed most fully by modern business, which is all about achieving results. As business has become more complex, the leadership challenge has grown form one of the simple issuing of orders to a few "hands" to the subtle coordination of highly skilled, diverse knowledge workers to build sophisticated machines and put men on the moon. There is a problem with this definition of leadership, however. It used to belong to management. Why the switch from management to leadership? And is this a good move? Up to the late 1970's writers used the terms leadership and management interchangeably but with more emphasis on management. For example, the management theorists, Blake and Mouton, developed their famous managerial grid in the 1960's. At the time, it was portrayed as a way of identifying your management style. Today, in line with the shift to leadership, the name is the same (managerial grid) but it is now positioned as a leadership style instrument.

Similarly, we used to talk about management style more than leadership style. Managers could be either "theory X" and task oriented or "theory Y" and concerned for people. But a profound shift in thinking took place in a revolutionary period lasting from the late 1970's through the mid 1980's. The cause of this upheaval was the commercial success of Japanese industry in North America. This led pundits to claim that the U.S. had lost its competitive edge because U.S. management was too bureaucratic, controlling, uninspiring and inept at fostering innovation. Rather than upgrade management, there was an emotional over reaction such that management was rejected and replaced by leadership. Since then, leaders were portrayed as theory Y, inspiring and concerned about people while management got saddled with all the bad guy attributes of being controlling, theory X, uninspiring and narrowly task focused. Similarly, the distinction between being transformational and transactional was originally launched to differentiate two leadership styles, but it wasn't long before it became used to separate leadership from management, the former being transformational and the latter transactional.

In our haste to trash management, we grabbed whatever tools were handy but with heavy costs. First, we painted leadership into a corner by suggesting that you needed to be an inspiring cheerleader to be a leader, leaving no room for quiet or simply factual leadership. Second, we created a bloated concept of leadership by banishing management. Third, by attaching leadership to getting things done through a team, we associated leadership irrevocably with being in charge of people, thereby ruling out positionless leadership. Yes, there is informal leadership but this concept is essentially the same as formal leadership except for their power bases. Like its formal counterpart, informal leadership still means taking charge and managing a group to achieve a target. In either case, you need to have the personal presence, organizational skills and motivation to take charge to be a leader.

Leadership means challenging the status quo, promoting a better way.

We have always felt, intuitively, that leaders have the courage to stand up and be counted. They go against the grain, often at great risk, to call for change. We only need to look at Martin Luther King, Jr. His leadership rested not so much on his oratorical skills - they were just icing on the cake. He was a leader primarily because he marched and spoke against injustice. He challenged the status ⬚uo and promoted a better world.

However, and this is the whole point here, if you think through what it means to challenge the status ⬚uo or advocate change, there is no necessary implication that you have to be in charge of the people you are trying to influence. The bottom line is that this third definition, when worked through fully, gives us a way to break the stranglehold of the previous two definitions. The benefit of this move is that we gain a clearer understanding of how all employees can show leadership even if they totally lack the skills or inclination to take charge of groups in a managerial sense, even informally. Think again of Martin Luther King, Jr. He sought to move the U.S. Government and the population at large to think differently about such issues as segregation on buses. His leadership efforts were successful when the U.S. Supreme Court ruled such discrimination unconstitutional. Now, it is obvious that he was not in a managerial role within the Supreme Court. He showed leadership to this group as an outsider. You could say the same of Jack Welch who had a leadership impact on countless businesses around the globe through his novel practices, such as being first or second in a market. Again, those who followed the lead of Jack Welch did not report to him. They were not even members of a common group.

Leadership Reinvented for the 21st Century

If we cast aside the first two definitions of leadership, what is left? If leadership means nothing more than promoting a better way, then we need to upgrade management to take care of everything to do with getting things done through people. We need to say that management does not entail being controlling, bureaucratic or theory X, that they can be as inspiring as they need to be, good at coaching, developing and empowering people.

A critical supporting fact is that the power on which leadership is based is shifting from having a dominant personality to the ability to devise new ways of working, new products and better services. Businesses that compete on the basis of rapid innovation are engaged in a war of ideas and no one has a monopoly on good ideas. This is revolutionary because it suggests that leadership can no longer be about group domination. Now, leadership is a brief influence impact, an episode or act, not an ongoing state or role. You still may need a larger than life personality to ascend to the role of Chief Executive, but leadership conceived as a good idea for a better way can be very small scale and local. Any employee with a better idea can promote it, even if only by example, without having the personal presence to be promoted to a managerial role. Strictly, speaking there are no longer any leaders, only leadership. This view captures the fact that leadership is a fleeting state that can shift quickly from one person to another. It is an impact rather than a type of person or position. It must be so if it can be shown by outsiders.

Key Features of Leadership Reinvented

It does not involve managing people to get things done.

It comes to an end once those led get on board. It sells the tickets for the journey; management drives the bus to the destination.

It is a discrete episode, a one-off act of influence, not an ongoing position of dominance.

It is based on the promotion of a better way.

It can be shown bottom-up as well as top-down.

It can be shown by outsiders and between competing individuals or groups.

Thought Leadership - The Essence of Leadership Reinvented

Organizations today need all employees to think creatively and to promote new products. Promoting a better idea can be called thought leadership. In a knowledge driven environment, the newest, best idea influences others to get on board. When a product developer convinces top management to adopt a new product, that person has shown thought leadership bottom-up. But it can be shown across groups as well. When Microsoft develops products or services invented by Apple or Google, they are following the lead of these innovators. This also is thought leadership.

While the possession of great emotional intelligence and the oratory of a Martin Luther King, Jr. can help thought leaders make their case, it is vital to see that these skills are nice to have add-ons, not an essential part of the meaning of leadership. Technical geeks with zero emotional intelligence and an obnoxious influencing style can show thought leadership if they can demonstrate the value of their ideas. This is very empowering because it moves us away from the demand to develop sophisticated leadership skills as a precondition of showing leadership. Strictly speaking there are no leadership skills, only influencing skills and great content. Imagine asking Tiger Woods. after the end of the third round when he is in the lead, how he developed such great leadership skills. The truth is that he shows leadership through being great at the content of his profession, not by having a separate set of talents called leadership skills. On the other hand, there are very definite management skills. Getting work done through people calls for quite sophisticated interpersonal and organizational skills.

Content is King

The point of the previous section is that convincing content or substance can trump great style or form. Having a larger than life personality may still help you get to be CEO but this is the power of style over substance. If the prospective leader has enough charisma, it almost doesn't matter what is being advocated (the content). Conversely, thought leadership is most convincing if backed up by hard evidence. Having persuasive influencing skills helps but isn't essential. This means that front line knowledge workers can focus on what it really takes to show leadership: begin by developing convincing content. If your idea is good enough it will virtually sell itself. It's not that influencing skills are not valuable. The point is that we can define leadership without mentioning influencing style. Also, there is the fact that opportunists will get on board with a great idea with no persuasion whatsoever. Thus, if it is possible to show leadership without being personally persuasive, then having such skills cannot be a necessary condition to show leadership.

The Future of Leadership

Leadership reinvented can still be shown by CEOs. They just need to accept that much of what they do needs to be reclassified as management. They also need to devote more time to fostering leadership in front line employees, thereby taking empowerment a huge leap forward. If they want to reap the full innovative potential of all employees, CEOs and other managers need to engage and inspire employees more fully. Helping them to see how all employees can show leadership now could make all the difference between winning the war of ideas and falling further behind. Where knowledge rules, the old fashioned conception of leadership as group domination is dangerously obsolete. Complexity drives specialization. It is time to bring management back from the dead to take care of getting things done through people, leaving leadership to focus on finding and promoting new directions.

Definition number 1 may still be good enough to capture what happens in small street gangs and primitive tribes but it is most clearly out of date in a world that is a war of ideas. Number 2 is a mess because it is a total confusion of leadership and management. Only definition number 3 captures all leadership - that shown by people in charge, by those with neither the inclination nor the skills to take charge, and by outsiders like Martin Luther King, Jr. UniＱuely, this definition also captures what it means to be a market leading company or a leading individual or team in sports. Leadership is simply a matter of showing the way. One of the many exciting features of this definition is that followers must choose to follow of their own free will because coercive power and authority are missing. Definition number 3 captures the essence of pure leadership.

Leadership Starts from Within

The global recession, directly or indirectly, will impact leadership - yours, your market, your competition, your region and, yes, your nation. Why?

Because leadership is ubiquitous. It is all around us. It is of primary importance. Yet, it is seemingly underserved, undervalued and under resourced. Need some proof?

According to the Development Dimensions International 's Global Leadership Forecast 2008/09 (1) from research of 1493 HR professionals and 12,208 business leaders across 76 countries:

75% of business leaders identified that improving or leveraging of leadership talent was their #1 priority.

Only 41% of business leaders are satisfied with the help they get to develop leadership capabilities.

One of the core needs within organizations is to create a sustainable supply of quality leaders.

The primary skill shortfall amongst organizations is in leadership skills and interpersonal skills.

Leadership is a leaking bucket. All organizations, large and small, from the family to local sport team to government to the boardroom of a leading global company, will at some time need to replace leaders. This arises from necessity and/or from natural attrition. From the information above, there is clearly a pervasive problem or, in a more positive tone, there is an opportunity - an opportunity to address this chronic shortcoming. How?

Start with yourself. Leadership starts from within.

To begin to explore this important distinction let's start by looking at the definition of leadership.According to the Oxford Dictionary leadership is the action of leading a group of people or an organization, or the ability to do this.

And...

To lead is to cause (a person or animal) to go with one by holding them by the hand, a halter, a rope, etc. while moving forward.

Leadership therefore requires influence, direction and action. However, for leadership to manifest so that others follow, it stands to reason that the leader, whoever or whatever that may be, must first influence themselves, give self-direction and act on that direction.

Chronic Question

There exists a perennial question about leadership - "Are leaders born or made?" or to rephrase it "Nature versus nurture".

Why does it need to be one or the other? Do you see many babies leading Fortune 500s or governments or the local sports team? Regardless of your opinion or perceptions one thing is for sure. Leadership is something into which you grow. Importantly, we are all born to lead ourselves at least!

In nature there must be reasonably synchronous growth regardless of the "ecosystem". Teenagers may experience growing pains when their bones are growing at a faster rate than their muscles. Our DNA is programmed so that eventually growth levels out and all systems are aligned and developed to their full design specification.

An individual promoted to a new role in an organization can experience a skill, attitude and/or ability gap compared to the new demands. To address the gap or deficit, the same individual must seek within first and begin the process of change there.

Admittedly, in organizations it is possible to experience growing pains too - sales and demand exceed the ability to supply and/or service the customer. Leadership must, therefore, develop within the organization to address the imbalance and ensure that harmony is restored.

What Does Google Have To Say?

As Google is the #1 search engine, it gives an impartial and objective perspective on leadership.

Just by typing in "leadership" yields 118 million results - sites, references etc. According to Google AdWords searches on the word "leadership" receives >4 million hits globally per month. Both of these facts suggest that leadership is a topic of significant interest and that there is a huge diversity of data, opinions, perceptions, models, styles, concepts and experts. The monthly searches also suggest there is a perpetual quest for answers, solutions and information on leadership.

Interestingly, when the global search is narrowed there are only:

4400 hits per month for "successful leadership"

33,100 hits per months for "effective leadership" and

18,100 hits per month for "self-leadership".

It is interesting that, in the face of all the need out there for leadership, the refined search on successful and effective leadership globally produces comparatively so few hits. Why is that? Is there a global delusion that we just need to know more about leadership or just understand it better rather than define what it takes to make a good leader or even a great one or to establish a legacy of outstanding leadership?

People - Your Most Important Asset

The mantra that people are your most important asset is spoken around the world. Too bad the mantra is wrong.

People are not your most important asset - the right people are. And that is especially true for the right leaders. The right leaders will attract, inspire, develop and retain the right people. The right leaders will be intent on growing other leaders. The right leaders will start by growing themselves - from the inside out. They know that to be a great leader they have to establish their own strong foundation of principles, values and attitudes.

A skills-based approach to leadership, however, takes an outside-in approach. That is where many individuals, teams and organizations get it wrong and contribute significantly to the statistics of the Global Leadership Forecast 2008/9. A skills approach to leadership assumes that good foundations have been laid upon which to lay the skills. To outright ignore examining and establishing the right foundation is in place is a huge risk. Regrettably, whether assumptions have been made or the matter outright ignored, this often equates, effectively, to throwing skills on Teflon. The result is skills will not stick.

Applying the skills-based approach, consider a formula for success, here applied to leadership, as Be x Do = Have. Have = good right leadership. Do = skills. Be =? Without addressing the 'Be' it is no surprise that leadership is chronically found wanting.

You get the people you deserve. It's your decision. For you to attract and lead better people you need to become the leader those people need and desire. That means you must invest in yourself first.

Where to Start

The majority of leaders should know and understand that people are the core building block of their team and/or organization. But to be an effective leader, you need to know the core building block of your people - their respective roles.

Many organizations just look at their people in their professional capacity. Whilst they may invest in their development and endeavour to lead them they often miss the mark. To ensure that your leadership "fits" and attracts the right people doing the right things to generate the right results, you need to ensure that you take into account all the roles each person comes to work with - within and outside the team or organization. This means you must address their personal roles outside of work e.g. parent, spouse, charity volunteer, team captain of local hockey team and coach of daughter's swim team (5 roles).

All of a person's roles show up at work. A leader is no different. They have as many if not more roles. The right leader will be addressing their growth and development in each role according to priorities and available "resources" (time, money etc.).

Self-leadership therefore begins by identifying core roles, prioritizing them, planning their development and then acting on the plan. To do all that it must begin from within.

Relationships

Interestingly, a leader will attract into their lives people and circumstances from which to learn and grow. Life is, after all, a mirror. The quality of your leadership is determined by the quality of your relationships.

There are two often quoted adages - love your neighbour as yourself and do unto others as you would have them do unto you. These both stress the importance of meaningful relationships and emphasize that all relationships start with you.

So leadership starts with your relationship with yourself. To improve your relationships with others so that you can become a better leader, you need to improve your relationship with yourself first. Regrettably, this revelation is often overlooked and/or not given the attention it is due.

A Critical Ingredient

Any relationship starts with you. Leadership starts with you. Self-leadership (and any leadership for that matter), to be effective, is dependent on the ability to communicate well - internally and externally. There is plenty of focus on external communication. For example, throughout the school systems around the world there is an emphasis regarding training around the messages from our mouth and from our pen or keyboard. However, what has been sadly overlooked is the greater importance of our internal communication.

All communication starts as a thought before it is translated into words and messages. How many of us have allowed ourselves to "speak first and think later"? What was the result? In many instances it likely created some unwelcome ripples in your life and in your leadership.

We all have an internal voice - actually we have two - our internal ally or our internal adversary. Our ally is working for us. Our adversary is working against us. As a leader which voice is loudest most often or to which one do you listen to most? When the adversary prevails it is often because we are reacting to a situation or challenge. Self-leadership knows to proactively and consciously control the voice to which it listens.

With self-leadership our internal (and external) communication must be open, honest, clear, timely and, at times, radical. Integrity then flows from this. When our thoughts line up with our words our actions will follow in alignment. We are congruent. We walk the talk. When we do that people do what people see. Your self-leadership then flows into leadership.

A Few Questions

To help initiate your self-leadership here are some extremely helpful questions for you to consider:

What is the detailed profile of the ideal leader for you, your team or your organization?

What are the foundations for self-leadership?

On a scale of 1-10 (1 being poor and 10 being excellent) how do you score on self-leadership?

In the event you did not score a 10 for #3 what do you need to be and/or do to improve your score to an 8+?

How do you encourage and develop self-leadership individually and/or as team or organization?

Where applicable, how will you integrate self-leadership into your existing leadership development?

PRACTICE, NOT THEORY.

Leadership is more about practice than theory, even if theory can inform some relevant insights as part of a leadership development program.

Leadership is a blend of art and science. Some leaders are born / pre-equipped better than others (nature), but intelligent training and development (nurture) can enhance virtually anyone's leadership capability.

Theories and models have a use, but only to underpin "practice" in leadership and real world outcomes.

Functional skills and previous performance are no guarantees of future leadership capability.

You will only get the leadership qualities that you select and train for.

The cost of promoting without leadership skills and then desperately seeking to equip people with adequate leadership skills can be high in human and economic terms.

Well-designed internal leadership academies can help when they match enhanced leadership awareness and capability to actual business needs.

For centuries much has been written about the "science" and the "art" of leadership.

Most of us have read and absorbed elements of this wisdom (and too often perhaps some of the come and go fads rather than wisdom). Many of us have subsequently pondered that age-old question about leadership; "are great leaders born, or are they made"?

Based on our experiences we have found that effective leadership capability tends to arise from a little of both in terms of settling that 'nature versus nurture' debate? Sabre's recent work on a number of high-level leadership academies (including one that was integral to the Coles turnaround) has confirmed that whilst there are many valid theories and models for the "science" of leadership, it's often the "art" of leadership that still evades adequate capture and definition.

Many businesses simply don't get it right, but it's reassuring to see those that do reap the positive rewards that flow so evidently from putting in the effort.

It is certain that nature does equip some people better than others in terms of their leadership traits (from a genetic, neurological and thence a behavioral perspective). There are those who just seem pre-loaded with healthy measures of IQ, charisma and also enough EQ to meld it all together in a way that gets their people to where they need to be.

Arguably though the honing of these skills that may at first glance seem to be gifted from "nature" can be attributed in at least part also to a degree of "nurture." For example, the development of complex neurological systems and patterns that drive much of our behavior (social systems of the brain, core belief patterns and embedded personality) can be traced to responses to external stimulus over the course of a lifetime.

It is however equally certain that proper approaches to 'nurture' can be used to raise the bar for virtually anyone who wishes to play the leadership game by enhancing awareness of their own strengths, areas of struggle and weakness as they manifest day to day.

Discipline is then required to act upon those insights of self-awareness to help cultivate better leadership capability for their own personal and professional circumstances.

One thing we often see is that being gifted in a particular functional skill or specialization, even to the point of genius, is no assurance that you can then lead a group of former peers in that field (or indeed any other).

Regular experiential "practice" of leadership comes into play as a valuable tool for enhancing the quotients of leadership talent that are gifted or acquired from our own recipe of nature and nurture. In the cut and thrust of day to day work life we don't always have adequate time to discern the true source of, and impact of our leadership and team role styles.

Current research and models from such emerging fields as neuroscience confirm some leadership theories and debunk others, and are often very useful in framing approaches and delivering ongoing insight. They are at the end of the day however just more tools for the toolbox, with leadership capability itself something that needs to be lived and developed day to day and powerfully linked to real world outcomes.

One of the clearest examples that I have observed was in the military when being selected for and subsequently entering into Army Officer training. Now whilst not all attributes of military leadership are relevant to commercial or non-military endeavours, it's safe to say that many are with respect to the human dynamics of leadership (particularly leading amidst complexity).

For Officer selection the emphasis was first and foremost upon personal leadership capability (and the potential to hone it further for a military environment). It was only much later after rigorous training in general military skills and leadership that relevant specialist streaming was done into various specializations and functional skills.

In commerce the reverse is often the case, where people are selected and promoted firstly with their "functional" skills and credibility strongly in mind (e.g. a great engineer, lawyer, stockbroker, salesman) with their leadership skills seldom given the same rigorous analysis as their functional results.

The Officer selection process was designed to reveal "leadership" potential first via a careful blend of psychometrics followed up with a host of mental and physical challenges that were rigorously observed by an experienced leadership selection panel. Their emphasis for selection was first upon core leadership traits exhibited under pressure, and the potential to polish those.

It was only much later that the aptitude for possible functional roles was to be explored. Functional experience and past performance, whilst taken into account if it was present, was never taken as an assurance of future leadership capability.

In commerce the best and brightest performer in a functional sense may not be the best person to lead a team of their former peers (unless they have been equipped by nature and nurture to lead also). The skills for leadership often exist outside of our functional skills, and are deserving of attention.

The military naturally values both individual leadership capability, and functional proficiency in an Officer's chosen trade post-graduation (e.g. Infantry, Armor, Artillery, Intelligence etc.), but the term "General Service Officer" is used to describe Army Officers upon graduation, and is used to imply that it's the "Officer" bit (your designated status as a leader) that comes first, and any functional / technical proficiency that may come later is second.

So much so that in theory any General Service Officer can be moved to or seconded into to virtually any military role or command should it be required of them. Of course you won't get far, or get much respect form peers or subordinates if you don't have some credible functional capability also, but the foundation is first your personal "leadership brand" which can be transferred into almost any other challenge.

Again, the military doesn't always get it right, but there is much to be said for the "leadership first" approach given to seeking and honing "Leadership DNA" as part of the overall process of developing organizational leadership talent. This in tandem with functional capability is ideal. Both matter, but the "personal leadership capability" bit is often overlooked in commerce (or considered as a clear second to ticking all the boxes on functional results and skills).

We have all seen people who are highly adept specialists in their given field (e.g. engineer, lawyer, doctor, stockbroker, IT professional) given leadership roles after getting runs on the board functionally speaking, without necessarily coming equipped with the requisite inter-personal and leadership awareness to handle the "non-functional" challenges of leadership.

Even being a respected genius at your chosen trade, does not ensure that you may end up out of your depth when asked to lead a cohort of your former peers (unless you have the "leadership bit" sorted first)?

The low morale, high turnover, friction and inefficiencies that can arise from poorly lead dysfunctional teams cost a great deal in both personal and economic terms This is where teams that on paper may have fall the boxes ticked for functional brilliance with their professional skills, experience and qualifications can simply fail through poor leadership and poor teamwork.

In a military environment the price paid for this is often instant, but in business it' can be slower and more insidious, but the outcome is the same, your team takes casualties and loses.

The ideal package for a leader is perhaps having enough functional proficiency to establish credibility, whilst also ensuring that they have been given ample opportunity to properly explore and develop their own leadership capability before being advanced to lead others. There is thus far less chance of being caught out of their depth in the all-important "leadership bit".

So how can business get the balance right?

The truth is that businesses can 'cherry pick' from the very best of the military approach by carefully designing and delivering their own internal leadership academies to target existing and emerging leaders. This enables people to build and develop upon existing leadership skills within the critical context of what they actually need to do and deliver within the business.

Time taken "outside" of the business, but very much "about" the business can really pay off when leadership development is tailored to meet business needs.

A person who possesses certain characteristics is capable of becoming a great leader. These characteristics can be learned by anyone who believes they are performing inadequately in their current position of leadership. An effective leader is someone who is able to successfully communicate assertiveness, confidence, leadership, responsibility and boldness.

Great leaders past and present often test positive for psychological traits such as these. If you were to break down the demands of each of these traits, you will become closer to understanding completely what it takes to become a more effective leader. In addition, a great leader must also be friendly, outgoing and good-natured. All of these characteristics are a major factor to becoming a more effective leader.

Research indicates that individual who possess traits such as these is typically happier, and people are more prone to follow someone who is in high spirits. An effective leader must be confident in his or herself. He or she must also be:

- Secure
- Self-reliant
- Certain
- Poised
- Brave
- Self-assured
- Fulfilled

Individuals who have high self-confidence are able to deal with challenges more successfully and are not discouraged easily. Effective leaders are better at handling unexpected events, making assertive judgments, and are able to articulate their opinions and thoughts quickly.

An effective leader is assertive; they must also be:

- Argumentative
- Influential
- Headstrong
- Persuasive
- Opinionated

When it comes to making decisions, an effective leader does not falter or hesitate, keeping the confidence of their followers. Becoming a good leader means that you know when something needs to be done, and you do not let anyone or anything stop you when you know you are right.

For many reasons, in order to lead effectively you must be bold. You must be able to keep your cool in unfamiliar territory, adapt to changes quickly and be willing to do whatever it takes to reach your goals and accomplish an overall objective. Bold leaders are more likely to prevail when there are tough decisions to be made.

In order to become a truly great leader, you must have a strong desire to influence, direct and control others. You must take on your role as a leader naturally and take pleasure in the challenges and responsibilities of being the one in charge. Your leadership style must be active, ensuring that you will take control quickly in any situation.

By making a commitment to study and make a conscious effort to learn the traits of an effective leader, anyone is able to improve and enhance their leadership skills. Not only will mastering the traits of a great leader help you become an expert in your industry, but can also help to improve your overall well-being.

Learn from Fellow Leaders

By following someone who is already an effective leader, you gain the experience and confidence that you need to become a leader yourself. A great many experts agree that anyone who wants to become successful in their business stand a better chance at it when you receive guidance from a mentor. A mentor has the type of wisdom that can only come from experience in the industry. When you are looking to climb the ladder of success and become an expert in your field, you would fare well from following in the footsteps of a great mentor.

Such a relationship will bring you valuable advice and guidance. You may benefit from having a mentor by attending events and meeting people that only those with mentor level experience are able to access. Mentors are more than happy to offer their guidance to subordinates because it gives them a chance to strengthen and improve on their own leadership skills and abilities.

Many businesses have failed because they underestimated the true value of a great mentor. A mentor can bring valuable insight and teach you a horde of useful things. Having great mentor in your life gives you peace of mind and comfort knowing that you have someone with knowledge of the industry that they are willing to share with you.

One advantage to having a mentor it they are able to encourage you and give you courage when you need that extra push. Others may offer encouragement to you, but when you hear it from a person who knows the ins and outs of your business it seems to have a greater meaning. A mentor can motivate you with nothing more than a straightforward comment affirming you that you are still on track, especially when you feel times are tough. Mentors have the ability to provide reassurance because they have experienced everything that you are going through on their own.

Gaining wisdom often comes from making mistakes. When you have a good mentor to follow, you are able to learn from their experience and avoid making the same mistakes with your business. Experience is the most effective lesson you will ever learn, but that experience does not have to be your own. You will save yourself a lot of time, money and heartache when you have a mentor helping you steer clear of the mistake that they made along the way.

You may form a great relationship with your mentor, but you do not necessarily have to be all that fond of him or her. You want a mentor who is a leader first and a friend last. A friend sees you for who you are while a mentor sees the person you are destined to become. A friend will simply accept your flaws and shortcomings, but a good mentor will not tolerate weakness.

A mentor will push you to be the professional expert that you know you can be. It takes a special kind of person to be able to draw the ability and talent out of less developed people. Talent is not just some skill that can be taught. A mentor is able to see the talent within and help you to bring out your best, and help you to discover special qualities you were not aware you had.

The main objective of a good mentor is to ensure your success; therefore, a good mentor is always willing to be truthful with you no matter what the situation may be. A mentor does not simply tell you what you want to hear. Telling you how great you are when you are wrong will never make you right.

A good mentor is invaluable for a number of reasons, such as providing:

Advice

Counsel

Encouragement

Knowledge

Motivation

A mentor is essential for your personal growth toward becoming a leader in your industry. In order to be an effective leader you must be able to follow the lead of someone who has already achieved great success in the industry.

BOTTOM LINE

Now, you know what it means to be an effective leader as well as the importance of being able to follow those who can teach you everything that you need to learn about your business. To be a true leader, you need to be able to influence others to be the best that they can be. As a leader, you must be an example for others to follow, as well as guide them and inspire them to achieve the goals that they have set for themselves.

Anyone can learn to lead. Each of us possess the potential for great leadership, just as we can all sing and dance. True some people are better at it than others are, but we can all build on the foundation with which we are born through practice, mentoring and training. You do not necessarily have to be born a natural leader to become a very effective leader.

Leadership is the course of action that assists a team in reaching its goals with success. Leaders and the other members of the team are able to have a mutual influence on one another's ideas. By exhibiting great leadership, one is able to find solutions that would otherwise go unknown. An effective leader is organized and possesses a harmonious combination of special behaviors, knowledge, skills and values that they are not only able to use for to achieve their own goals, but to also aid others in doing the same. Everyone has his or her own beliefs of the different traits that a valuable leader should have.

Each team is different when it comes to values and beliefs about what is considered an effective leader. The team will assess the leadership skill of the candidate and decide on a leader based on how the traits compare to the characteristics that particular team finds valuable. It is vital that you are aware of your own knowledge, values and abilities as well as what others think of you.

For instance, if creativity is a highly valued characteristic for the team, then it is crucial that you be seen as a creative person. When you are completely aware of your own weaknesses and strengths, you will also be able to create a plan to work on the areas in which you may need a little improvement.

If you intend to successfully become a more effective leader, you must make an effort to practice and learn the skills. A few of the most important components are:

The ability and skills to communicate successfully

Building teams

Vision

The ability to add value to individuals and the team

Taking risks

Understanding and knowledge of specifics

Basic knowledge about your business, how to run an effective meeting and to efficiently take care of business are typical characteristics of a good leader. An effective leader is well aware of the business, its purpose, goals and objectives. A good leader knows that they cannot successfully achieve their objective on their own. The notion that the leader is above the others in a team is a thing of the past.

An efficient leader is fully involved in the team's projects and stays in contact with the members of the team. A truly valuable leader will enable the members of the team to reach their objectives by offering emotional support, technical assistance and total vision. A good leader will insist on the assistance and support of everyone influenced by the project.

One of the greatest characteristics of an effective leader is that they take the time to reward and recognize the members of their team for a job done well. When the members of the team are bored, frustrated and tired with a certain goal, task or project, they may be tempted to throw in the towel and call it quits. It is the responsibility of the leader to motivate and encourage the group to continue with the project through completion.

Expressing genuine respect and concern for the business, the community and all the people affected is a sure fire strategy to achieving expert status in the industry. You will not find a special recipe or magic spell to turn you into an effective leader. You must endure the trial and error process and never quit learning and practicing until you are the successful leader that you know you can be.

Leadership and Integrity - Ensuring it Exists in Your Company

There has been a steady rise in the awareness of employees, shareholders, and the general public of serious lapses in good governance and corporate ethics. One needs look no further than the newspapers to read about the misfortunes of large, high profile corporations, quasi-governmental agencies, and non-profit organizations. In the last 4 to 5 years, we have been inundated with the likes of Enron, Hollinger, WorldCom, Boeing, Freddy Mac, and even the American Red Cross. It seems companies just can't get it right.

There are now increasing demands on members of the Board of Directors in companies to take steps to 'avoid risk', to be more 'aware' of how the company is managed and to do 'risk analysis'. The current trend in measuring the quality of governance in organizations is to measure their success in applying good governance principles at the Board level. However, we must remember that members of the Board do not lead or manage an organization on a day-to-day basis and the overall general 'health' of the organization's integrity and ethics rests in the hands of the managers inside the company. Boards ask for reports. But where do those reports come from?

This is an important concept that bears repeating. The overall general 'health' of the organization's integrity and ethics rests in the hands of the managers inside the company - every day. I know the companies we've been reading about had policies - that's standard practice, a must! But simply having a policy won't instill integrity or consistently ethical behaviour in an organization.

What consistent or common thread exists in the news reports we read on these companies? The fundamental issue is the lack of demonstrated ethics and Leadership integrity. These have become lost treasures where they are not consistently and deliberately reinforced by example and through systems and programs. Strategic Human Resources management can build programs and processes that continually reinforce and reward integrity throughout the organization.

One thing effective leaders have in common is a strong set of core values and among the top values you will find ethics and integrity. Strong leaders use their core values as a set of guiding principles or a moral compass. If they work for someone else, they understand the need to ensure that the corporations' and their core values are in sync. If they are starting a new company or working in a start up, they know they must establish and communicate these values. These values will be the center of the corporate culture and if used properly will reduce risk and increase productivity and profitability.

But in the face of the constant news of unethical behaviors in companies around the world, one might well ask, "Where have all the strong leaders gone?" Companies need to, and should, focus on sales and profit, but if those are the only considerations the organization can become sociopathic in its focus - to the exclusion of doing what's right for the company, employees and customers.

Even good leaders can succumb to the profit driven sociopathic culture. Overcome by exceptions to policies and ill-defined compensation plans, they begin to believe that success is profit, no matter how attained. We've seen it happen. Yet sustainability cannot be achieved through profitability alone and great leaders know this. Great leaders work to build a culture that requires ethics and integrity in all actions; and if they are unable to do this, they leave.

Human Resources as an Integrated Business System

While some companies utilize their Human Resources staff to the fullest, others have failed to realize that HR can impact the bottom line positively. Worse still, they miss the mark by not looking for strategically minded HR staff to use as a key resource in the battle to reinforce Integrity and Ethical behaviors throughout the organization.

If the Human Resources role is expected to be a business support system in the same way as Finance or IT, it can be a powerful tool. There are internal and external influences that HR staff deals with on a daily basis. However, HR as a business system, whose processes, policies and programs are built around the corporate value system is something to behold.

Recruiting & Selection

Looking for individuals who not only subscribe to the corporation's values and but also have integrity and are ethical is critical. If you hire for these behaviors your life becomes simpler right off the bat. I often hear people say "but how do I know if these people are a good fit until I work with them?"

Behavioral interviewing is the best approach to finding people that fit an organization culture of any I have used in my career. Anyone participating in the interview process in an organization should be trained in this process. Instead of looking only at technical skills, interview teams can ask well-designed questions that will gather information in these areas. You need to seek information on both technical and behavioral skills and experience in order to find well-rounded individuals. By doing this, you will select individuals with high levels of integrity and proven ethical behavior. This is the first step to reducing risk.

Performance Management

Once you have people in place you need to reinforce behaviours by measuring them. Incorporating the values into the performance management system will do that. It also becomes a communication vehicle and an opportunity to send the message continually. It would be perfect to start a company using this process. If the company is already an entity, the performance management system can communicate the values to existing staff and identify those whose values are not in sync with the company's. The reality is that these people may have to leave.

Compensation & Rewards

If people do well in their performance assessment on their technical competence - we give them a raise. Measure their contribution on values and behavior as well and let have that impact the amount of their increase and you will get their attention. What if, for example, you have a great sales person who exceeds plan every year but leaves dead bodies in his or her wake internally because they treat team members badly? Identify this in a performance review and hopefully the individual will improve. If there is no improvement you have documentation that is the beginning of a termination process. Terminate a star sales person?! I know this sounds like lunacy but consider the impact that person has on productivity not to mention the cost to hire and train new staff.

Build a feedback survey process into the performance assessment to ensure decisions regarding pay are made with a broad view of the individuals' performance.

Design incentive plans that build checks and balances into the calculations and reward only for the right business. Definitions should include words regarding the kind of business and be specific about how it is gained in keeping with corporate values.

Career & Succession Planning

A bad hire costs money to terminate or replace but the damage that person can do in terms of how employees view the company is phenomenal. Promoting a bad hire or someone that isn't demonstrating the values, compounds the issue and sends a clear message to employees. It is critical to continually assess the behaviors of your high potentials. Leadership surveys, regarding values and 'walking the talk' should be conducted annually, making career and succession decisions clear.

Employee Communication

This is by far the most critical aspect to utilizing an HR Business support system to it's fullest.

Communicate, communicate, communicate!! Never miss an opportunity to talk about expectations, good work contributing to goal attainment, behaviours that support the corporate culture, and employees that set good examples.

Great Leaders take every opportunity to reinforce the right stuff!

Effective Time Management As a Leader

A strategic way to boost your business leadership results, along with its profits, productivity and growth is through effective time management practices. Because time, as it is in any profession, is a critical resource in making business leadership actions profitable, innovative and transformative.

Before we continue, you need to appreciate this important fact about business leadership - whether we're talking about market, innovative, strategic, situational, transformational, project or organizational leadership - leadership in any form is always a social activity.

So with that understanding, we can look at business leadership in three generic ways: as market leadership, organizational leadership and human capital leadership.

In business organizations, entrepreneurs may choose to invest their time in human capital related leadership activities, that is in leading, coaching or soliciting and recruiting the support of their associates and trading partners.

Entrepreneurial leaders also have opportunities to use their time to contribute to the quality, quantity or significance of life for their customers and clients. I call these actions a form of market leadership.

Business leadership tasks demand that leaders analyze, plan and re-order their budgets, cash flows, operational systems or their schedules, where their sole objective is to manage their time as profitably, effectively and creatively as possible. We can call these activities organizational leadership.

A fact-of-life for those professionals charged with business leadership responsibilities - which includes the executives, entrepreneurs and managers - they will usually encounter the most disruptions, interruptions or other forms of distractions to their scheduled activities. Unfortunately, in the face of that reality, these business leadership personnel tend to immediately discount, ignore or underestimate the potential value in those unanticipated events.

If you ever hope to become an effective leader you should never focus your attention on the management of accomplishing tasks against a daily allotment of your time, you should however concentrate your energies on the management or maximizing the allocations of your significance.

We know that being effective means doing the right things. We also know that being efficient is doing things the right way. Are you doing the "right things" or are you doing things "the right way"?

The problem with the focus of most time management strategies is this, we are told to be efficient in our use of time, that is, we're taught that the right way of doing time management is to plot whichever tasks we feel or believe we need to accomplish in a certain amount of time segments.

And in the case of business leadership, the right things for your usage of time must be based upon your contributions of ⬚uality, ⬚uantity or the value of your significance.

In a word, your contributions have to be acts that you take for the purpose of being of benefit to all the actors, artifacts or artifices, attributes and audiences engaged in your social activity. On the other hand, your significance must add a form of excellence, emphasis, essence, elevation, eminence, effectiveness, efficacy, efficiency, execution, elucidation, explanation, exposition, expression or esteem to your actions.

"Most executives, many scientists, and almost all business school graduates believe that if you analyze data, this will give you new ideas. Unfortunately, this belief is totally wrong. The mind can only see what it is prepared to see." - Edward de Bono, creativity expert

I advise my business leadership clients to keep strategic ⬚uestions in mind whenever they engage in any activity. I call these mini-evaluations strategic because being strategic means being decisive, deliberate and dexterous - meaning leaders who wish to be strategic thinkers or questioners have to think through, think about and think with their actions, don't they?

The purpose of those ⬚uestions isn't to generate answers consisting of one-word or a single idea. And leaders shouldn't use these questions to judge a moment-in-time as being either significant or worthless. Rather than making those types of value judgments, these ⬚uestions should ensure you have competent, strategic responses prepared, organized and ready to go in advance, so that you can optimize, leverage or otherwise make the best use of those planned-for or unplanned-for periods of time.

Here is one set of example ⬚uestions you could ask to help you make more effective use of your time, regardless of any interruption, or unexpected or distracting event.

"Never permit a dichotomy to rule your life, a dichotomy in which you hate what you do so you can have pleasure in your spare time. Look for a situation in which your work will give you as much happiness as your spare time." - Pablo Picasso, artist

(Can I Make This) Quality Time?

Is it pure? [resulting in no distractions, disruptions, delays from your goals or mission]

Is it sweet? [warm, refreshing and enjoyable experience or environment or forum or venue]

Is it absolute? [secure, or obligated to my relationship, or persuasive or memorable]

"We need to internalize this idea of excellence. Not many folks spend a lot of time trying to be excellent."

- USA President Barack Obama

(Can This Moment Become) Quantity Time?

Is it substantial? [is there substance, meaning or fulfillment in this use of my time?]

Is it concrete? [producing a specific, tangible, measurable, realistic, attainable result from the use of my time]

Is it clear? [does it help me be or become more focused, intentional, results-driven, practical]

Or you could use dimensionally-oriented questions to determine, implement and supervise your applications of business leadership significance. As we mentioned earlier, time can be measured against a location - that is, time and a location in space are always related - so we say, "you are always somewhere at some specific point of time!"

"Between stimulus and response there is a space. In that space is our power to choose our response. In our response lies our growth and our freedom." - Viktor E. Frankl, psychologist

In the social expanse known as "space-time", you'll discover how dimensional constructions usually hold true. Social dimensions include the scope, importance, direction, magnitude, definition, quantity, aspect, extent, element, a position, attribute, property or proportion of any social activity.

Dimensional characteristics are important because they provide insights into the breadth, depth, thickness and heights of your utilization of time - are your capital assets being transformed into something tangibly significant, are your human players moving together in harmony, are the reasons for pursuing this action realizing the desired results?

Therefore, you will need to ask the following types of questions to generate the right types of dimensionally important answers and thus understand how well or how effectively you are using your time for performing your business or organizational leadership tasks:

Where-When: describes a physically obvious, tangible reality of an event without trying to explain any aspect of human, social or physical capital involvement or influences;

Who-What: defines and describes the moving parts, functional attributes and players of human exchanges, transactions, interactions or reactions

Why-How: endeavors to provide causes or reasons for human actions and seeks to identify the ways and means employed to satisfy or attain the desires for taking those actions

We can easily describe the process of how and when to take action to use the extant sources and depth of information, which are what you have, to help you become what you desire, to unleash the future envisioned by what your dreams have awakened within you, and prosecute your strategy for business leadership to the ultimate extent of your resources, expertise and abilities.

"Dream and give yourself permission to envision a You that you choose to be." - Joy Page, actress

However, in essence, we must look at each and every one of our competitive, operational and developmental efforts as activities taking place within, and, as actions existing at points along, positions within or locations of "space-time" - that is, using these reference placements to indicate, investigate or interrogate the:

Manifold - Which diverse, variety and many features of my actions...?

Affect or Add-to the Dimensionality - the ins and outs, ups and downs, across and around, over and under, back and forth, breadth and length, brokenness and wholeness, heights and depths - of our efforts...?

Time-frame - When will or When must the intervals, periods, moments, phases, ages, eons, ticks occur and...?

Relativistic - How or How much does it relate to our past, present or future perspectives...?

Who benefits or is impacted by the Attractions, Interactions, Transactions or Reactions of our informed actions - and Why will they be...?

Thus in the realm of social phenomena, we define "space-time" as the distinctive features and structural dimensions which identify the cognitive, cultural or emotive segments of perspectives and interactions involved when we act, acted or will take action.

"But the best teams I've encountered have one important thing in common: their team structure and processes cover a full range of distinct competencies necessary for success." - Jesse James Garrett, Infopreneur, information architect

Therefore, business leadership means incorporating the "physics" of socially-oriented space-time into the creation and application of a much more effective time management program to generate profitable results and strategic innovative opportunities while it strengthens your organizational leadership development programs and performance improvement efforts.

Struggling to Build a Successful Team? Leadership Development Methods

"Leaders are born, not created," true... maybe.

Strong leadership skills are taught and nurtured just like many other capabilities. Perhaps your company has not done a good job creating effective leadership development programs. This article gives you the most important leadership aspects to grow your business.

This article is also useful if you are the leader of your own creative business.

Throughout my coaching programs, I stress the importance of keeping your team members involved. Building a team means you keep recruits responsive, engaged, and energetic about the business.

Above all, this principle is the most important aspect to a successful business. Even more important, I believe, than recruiting.

Why?

You can recruit thousands of team members. You can spend all day, every day recruiting. But if those members lose interest and quit, then you are spending your time in vain.

I encourage you to recruit with the end goal of supporting your team. And this goes for as many people you sign up (small or large numbers).

Leadership Development: Host Live Team Trainings

There is a certain level of fear when you realize you have just sponsored a team member. Now it is up to you to teach them how to be successful. In fact, this fear is what keeps many people from being successful in their business. They refuse to learn how to train other team members. I have heard the excuse "How can I teach someone when I am not successful yet myself?" The best response I give? Get over the fear. Every leader once started exactly where you are now! Leaders had to step up into a role they may not have been comfortable with at that moment.

Leaders look to build a performance driven, direct sales team that delivers results. Plain and simple.

The only way to achieve this goal is to start hosting live team trainings every week. It is not enough to send your new recruits to the weekly company call, or to send them to their back office. They need you! There are some amazing (and free) live video services that you can use to host your own live trainings. I encourage you to get online today and find a service that suits your needs.

Training your own team will be a huge factor in developing your leadership skills.

Once you achieve a weekly training schedule, I encourage you to teach your up and coming leaders. Teaching your down line leaders to train will prove invaluable to your whole organization.

Here is an example of a problem that live trainings will solve:

You have just sponsored a person onto your team. But, they were mistaken and thought they could 'get rich' by signing up and not working. Live trainings teach them how to work without forcing them to do anything more than "show up".

Your basic responsibility as team leader is to support individual team members. A one-on-one relationship recognizes and encourages good performance. Its principle objectives are improving well-being, resolving problems, and developing the team member.

Your end goal is to have a personal relationship with each team member. But not to become so overwhelmed that you have no time left to keep building your personal business.

Solution:

Weekly live trainings. As the leader, you must be available to have training for at least a half hour every week. This will include question and answer time. Every week your team will recognize that you are there to support them. The team grows when new members can join the training and support already in place.

As the leader (at ANY level) you have a responsibility to assist and develop team members. Remember, first you are a trainer and teacher. As leader, counseling your team members is necessary to keep them motivated and expanding.

Leadership Development: Maintain a strong personal business, a large team, and still enjoy life!

Being the leader of your team is going to come with some adjustments on your part.

One of the largest adjustments you are going to make is to your mentality. The only person responsible for your success is you. The only way to be successful is to have a successful attitude. Your attitude makes all the difference to the survival and success of your team. Your business, and team success depends on your mentality.

Leadership Development Questionnaire:

1. As the leader of my team, do I have a passion for the products?

_____

2. Do I have passion for the business opportunity? What has this business opportunity given me in my life that I did not have before?

_____

_____

3. Does my charisma and joy for the business overshadow any stress, time commitment, and unforeseen obstacles I will face while supporting my team?

_____

_____

As with any job, (a traditional corporate 40 hour a week or our self- run business), we want to have a satisfying experience. Building your large team will come with its own stress, so how do you continue to enjoy your life while you are building this foundation in the beginning? The answer is you must be a true believer.

You are the true believer in your business. There is no room for the skeptic or cynic. Only with passion will persistence and patience occur. And with those two attributes you will be a successful leader inside of your team. It is rare that a direct sales leader experiences overnight success. It will be your attitude, passion, patience, and persistence that will be the defining factor on whether or not you will build a large team, while still enjoying the process and ultimately, your life.

Leadership Development: Which systems will streamline the time commitment in your business?

As with any job, a corporate 40 hour a week or our self- run business), we want to have a satisfying experience. Building your team will come with its own stress. So how do you continue to enjoy your life while you are building this foundation in the beginning? The answer is you must be a true believer.

You are the true believer in your business. There is no room for the skeptic or cynic. Only with passion will persistence and patience occur. And with those two attributes you will be a successful leader inside of your team. It is rare that a direct sales leader experiences overnight success. It will be your attitude, passion, patience, and persistence that will define your success. These factors determine whether you build a large team while still enjoying your life.

Leadership Development: Which systems will streamline the time commitment in your business?

As with the previous topic, your goal is to build a strong business with a large downline team. This process can become so time consuming that you spend your life wrapped up in growing the business. When this occurs, you will see that you have not become any different than an all-consuming 9-5 job.

To build a large and motivated team, but enjoy your life, here are your business efficiency tips.

1. Outsource as much as you can. Only focus on core responsibilities.

Today you can outsource non-essential responsibilities to a virtual assistant. As leader, your goal is to one day completely run your business on automation. A core responsibility is to create training material for your team and teach them once a week. As your team grows larger you can increase this training time. Outsource what you do not need to be spending valuable mental energy on. There are millions of people at your fingertips to write your blog content for you (and for cheap). You can have a virtual assistant track all your social media comments and respond for you. Spend a couple bucks and have automation tools post content to your social channels. Completely hands-free while you focus on core goals.

Outsource any time consuming activity that you are not passionate about. You will laugh at exactly what you can outsource! This saves your sanity and passion for what matters. Recruiting and supporting your team.

What can you outsource today: _____

_____

Invest your time in building your own system for team support. What works for the larger company, might not work for you and your personal goals. Take time now to develop a strategy for supporting your team. This will save you effort in recruiting people who just ⬚uit.

Expect Emergencies. Tip number one was outsourcing as much as possible. This prepares you for an emergency, which will happen. When it does your business keeps running while you deal with the emergency. Keeping your workload streamlined means when the unexpected occurs, you are still productive.

What is one emergency you could see happening? What process would you have in place to overcome and keep your sanity: _____

_____

_____

Leadership Development: Coaching and training... Why you must host both in your business

Coaching:

As the team leader, if you fail to coach, you failed to fulfill a major leadership responsibility.

Coaching your down line team, means focusing on how well they are performing. You offer up praise, give them success strategies, help, and guidance. (Even if you had to pay for it yourself!)

On an inherent level, your team expects to hear how they are doing. They need to feel welcome to ask questions from you. They want to hear your experience and knowledge. This one-on-one relationship will foster individual growth.

It is an absolute rule that as the leader, you coach (this is where the weekly Q & A comes into play) your team members.

Training:

Team training should focus around 2 different styles:

Directive:

The directive approach to training is leader-centered. Directive training is simple, ⬚uick, and provides solutions to problems.

As leader, you have all the skills and knowledge to offer courses of action. Use suggestion, persuasion, and next step action plans to achieve results.

You will do most of the talking in directive training. Define problems, causes, give advice, and solutions. You will find that most team members prefer this type of training.

Non-Directive:

The non-directive approach to training is individual-centered. As leader you encourage the team to be responsible for solving their own problems.

Non-directive training is ideal for team members who want responsibility for their own business. They do not like following the crowd and prefer to make their own decisions.

Leadership Development: Keys to successful leadership

Leadership Development: Keys to successful leadership

The most significant action to build a great team involves refining your leadership skills. Amazing leadership skills allow you to address immediate team member problems. As your business grows, leadership qualities positions yourself for a successful business.

KEY #1: Directing and motivating people.

Ask yourself, "Do I have the passion to coach, motivate, and train my team 30 minutes (or more) once a week?"

_____

KEY #2: Strategic Planning - translating vision into realistic business strategies, including long-term objectives.

Take time today to create a strong vision that leads your team toward a positive future. Share that vision with all team members. Clearly state where you are going and how you plan to get there.

KEY #3: Inspiring Commitment - recognizing and rewarding team member's achievements.

As team leader, nurture loyalty and commitment by knowing what motivates your team. This includes recognition, communication and other activities. Build your leadership skills by recognizing team member achievements (no matter how small). Share a clear vision and connecting it to your team member's goals. Recognizing, rewarding and celebrating successes. Setting a high goal for the whole team to achieve.

KEY #4: Doing whatever it takes - persevering despite the current condition.

If you want to be a successful leader, you will have to be authentic.

Your team will stay dedicated and motivated if they feel your genuine commitment. The team needs to believe what you say.

Be self-aware. Understand your strengths and weaknesses. Listen to other ideas, this supports your team.

KEY #5: Being a Quick Learner - Quickly learning new technical or business knowledge.

Seek feedback from not only team members, but coaches and other mentors.

Align your business and leadership strategies by making sure that your business plans and team development strategies are in line with current (and productive) strategies.

Be On top of your game

When speaking on leadership, so many typical conversations occur such as being responsible or educated, but the fact is that there are many people out there that are highly skilled and educated, responsible to the core and possess a high ethical and moral value system that cannot lead. It happens time and time again, a person of great skill in a company is promoted due to their exceptional results, only to fail as a manager or team leader. So there has to be more to leadership then these elements. After doing some research, these qualities are what I found often are common amongst leaders: Inspirational, good listening skills, ability to forecast, and courage to act.

Leadership is lifting a person's vision to higher sights, the raising of a person's performance to a higher standard, the building of a personality beyond its normal limitations. It is not magnetic personality, that can just as well be a glib tongue. Leadership is getting someone to do what they don't want to do, to achieve what they want to achieve. It is about making other leaders and not followers. To do that, one must recognize the strengths in others and then nourish them. In projects that can allow for a little time and guidance, do not put your best man on the job. Put your second best man on the job and guide him to a number one performance. When you take others under your wing and nourish them to become leaders, you grow a team you can count on to make decision in your absence. This inspiration to be more then what one currently is not only builds self confidence in the individual, it builds investment in the company providing that leadership. An employee vested in the success of your company for personal reasons will perform at a much higher level then the one strictly motivated by the dollar amounts in his paycheck.

Get in there, roll up the sleeves and lead by example if deadlines are difficult or staff is short. There is nothing more inspiring to have your boss at your side sweating out the details rather then just expecting the results on his/her desk the next morning. This is not a new concept in the world of business and politics. Even John Quincy Adams stated, "If your actions inspire others to dream more, learn more, do more and become more, you are a leader." However to do this, to help others be even more then what they realize they are capable of you must have the second skill, good listening.

Active listening is one of those skills that's both surprisingly simple as well as surprisingly effective. It should include allowing others to make a point before interrupting, and valuing the opinions of others. In addition to improving your personal and professional relationships, listening also helps to prevent misunderstandings and facilitates cooperation. A great listening technique involves rephrasing the speaker's words and repeating them back to them. This shows that you are listening and are following them. Pay attention to what they are not saying as well as what they are. Sometimes a leader can pick up things to guide with by what the person is avoiding bringing up due to a lack of comfort in that particular subject area. Pay attention to the body language of the speaker. Does their posture show true intent or are they just speaking to hear themselves talk. When you respond, are their arms folded across their chest? This is a common defensive posture. There are many good books and seminars out there on communication skills, make sure to use one that includes active listening. One I recommend is Active Listening: Improve Your Ability to Listen and Lead (J-B CCL (Center for Creative Leadership)) Without this skill, you are not truly hearing the needs of important people in your life or business team and therefore, cannot take appropriate action.

Again, this not a new idea or a new revelation to business and relationships. Epictetus from 55 - 135 AD is quoted as saying. "We have two ears and one mouth so that we can listen twice as much as we speak." Unfortunately, the competitive nature often jumps into conversations and we become focused on winning a point or making ourselves heard and we lose the concept of open-minded and receptive. An important aspect of good communication as well as personal growth.

Another important aspect of leadership is the ability to forecast. On a larger scale, businesses are forced to look well ahead in order to plan their investments, launch new products, decide when to close or withdraw products and so on. Often, the financial well-being of the entire operation rely on the accuracy of the forecast since such information will likely be used to make interrelated budgetary and operative decisions in areas of personnel management, purchasing, marketing and advertising, capital financing, etc. What often gets overlooked is what will the employees need to meet the ever changing needs of the company. Is there training on new concepts that are needed. Is the time taken to educate the employees on the reasons for the change and the positive end results. One mistake often made in business is to throw change at employees with a 'just do it' mindset. However, if employees or even children for that matter, understand what is to be gained in the change and what the impact to them personally will be; they will be better able to manage the change and move forward in a positive manner.

One of the most important skills is the ability to make a decision, to take action. Often in today's world, untrained leaders are put into positions to make decisions they do not feel empowered to make. A leader forecasts the end results of a decision and makes it. It is often heard by frustrated employees, "will someone just make a decision." Leaders make decisions and stand by them. If they make a mistake, they own them and learn from them then move on. By role modeling decision making, you teach others to do the same. Wherever possible, give people the power to make decisions and learn. Face it, most of us got our best learning experiences when we fell flat on our faces. By listening to what is going on and monitoring our teams, we can intervene before such mistakes our disastrous to the company over all. A mentor of mine is always saying - "trust but inspect." That is our role as a leader, to teach and inspire others to reach for the stars. As they reach, we guide their progress and help them analyze their results.

People do not have to be born leaders. They can learn to lead. Take the time to listen to those that are where you want to be. Forecast your decisions and possible end results before making decisions then look at who you need to achieve that path. Inspire others by being the person, the team player, that you want them to be. In other words, don't sit back and tell what is to be done, show what needs to be done. Roll up your sleeves and be willing to stand side by side on the sales floor, the copy room or even the mail room if there is a need and a shortage. Not only will it show your leadership skills and that you care for the team you lead, it will allow you to hear new ideas and spot problems quicker, it will allow you to find your future leaders as they step up beside you.

5 BIG Mistakes

The 5 BIG Mistakes that organizations make when developing their leadership talent is costing them in productivity, staff engagement, staff satisfaction and staff retention; never mind the escalating costs of replacing individuals and getting them up to speed to do an effective job.

As you read through these 5 BIG Mistakes - and the problems they create - you'll immediately be in a position to introduce new strategies to develop your leadership talent, increase engagement and reduce those costs associated with employees being disengaged and leaving your company for "greener pastures". In fact, continuing to do what the industry has always done will continue to get you the same results. Many of the standard old and tired approaches to leadership development simply don't work and fail to deliver on organizational (and employee!) expectations. It's time to take a new approach.

Every organization wants them and every organization says they're committed to building them but how many organizations actually produce great leaders at every level throughout their business?

There are many benefits of having leaders, including self-leaders, at every level of the organization and some of these include:

Proactivity: The ability to set and achieve our own objectives.

Accountability: Taking responsibility for our mistakes and making them right.

Motivation: That drive that gets us to the office early and keeps us focused throughout the day.

Confidence: Being able to present new ideas and having the self-assurance in ourselves and our capabilities.

Harmonization: Being a team player, making decisions and acting in-line with organizational values.

Enthusiasm: Having the energy and "juice!" to overcome any challenges we come across.

Inspiration: The ability to move people toward a cause that is greater than themselves.

Self-awareness: Understanding ourselves, our strengths, our weaknesses and taking on the challenge of becoming better.

#1: Employees will pick up leadership skills on the Job...

If you want to be a great leader the best way to become one is to get close to an individual who already demonstrates great leadership practices. Stick with them as much as you can, learn everything you can from them, observe them, especially in the tough times; get to know how they think and how they make decisions. Most importantly, identify those unique character traits that set them apart and work on developing those within yourself.

That's the ideal way... regrettably most organizations lack great leadership in the first place and there is a shortage of good leadership role-models. Unfortunately, when people are asked about 'leadership' they tend to think 'management'.

Start developing real leadership skills in your organization now and reverse this trend!

Another unfortunate aspect of organization culture is that there is no incentive to developing leaders; therefore, we are more concerned about getting the job done rather than spending the time needed with our people to help them grow. We are too busy in our day to day jobs to realize that by developing our teams they will experience the confidence to step up and take on many of the day to day tasks that prevent you, a leader of people, from focusing on where you can add value most. Most leaders don't have the skill-set to do this because they have never experienced it themselves and lack the knowledge of how to apply it to others.

Bill O'Brien, former president of Hanover Insurance in the United States argues that managers must redefine their job. They must give Bill O'Brien up "the old dogma of planning, organizing and controlling," and realize "the almost sacredness of their responsibility for the lives of so many people." Managers' fundamental task, according to O'Brien, is "providing the enabling conditions for people to lead the most enriching lives they can.

Developing a great leadership culture doesn't happen by chance. It takes time, effort and focus. It takes an understanding of the core leadership competencies and embedding these into the organizational culture where they are measured and reviewed.

Learning leadership is like a quest - there's no defined path to success. It's a personal journey and is different for everyone.

Identify where your leaders are spending their time. Is their focus on developing their people or managing the things their people do?

Believing that employees will learn on the job without a dedicated leadership culture in place will lead to disappointment and frustration for all involved.

The task of leadership is not to put greatness into humanity, but to elicit it, for the greatness is already there.

How are you going to start developing your people rather than manage them? What activities can you let go of and give to an aspiring team member to free up your time and contribute to their growth?

What are the leadership objectives for your team members or yourself? Remember, leadership is about leading yourself first! What changes can you make in your life to become a real leader?

#2: Sending employees on 2 or 3-day leadership training courses...

If you've ever been on a 2 or 3-day training course I've no doubt that you learned a lot of valuable information and that the course was a great buzz... a fantastic cerebral hit! You've probably come away from the course motivated to make loads of changes and become a truly great leader.

But what happens when you get back to your desk? Generally, there are hundreds of unread emails waiting for your urgent attention. That little light on your phone is blinking away telling you have several phone messages also waiting for your urgent attention. Don't forget about your team... They've been fighting the fires while you were away and now they all need a decision on this and a decision on that. Soon those valuable lessons you learned during those two or three days recede into distant memory and you never get the opportunity to make any real and lasting change.

Organize your training in a series of short hits over a period of weeks to allow time for practice and feedback.

Apart from the inconvenience of being out of the office for two or three days at a time and never really being able to shut off to give the material the attention it deserves, does the core content actually deal with real leadership competencies?

Real leadership stems from character and the thing with character is that it can't be developed in a couple of days... no matter how well the material is delivered. When I mentioned above that most courses are a 'fantastic cerebral hit' I wasn't exaggerating. Intellectually they are very stimulating but that's the problem.

You see, most people know the competencies of great leaders but very few know how to develop those traits that makes them stand apart. If it was as simple as understanding these traits we'd all be leaders but unfortunately this is not the case. It's not the case because the area of the brain that is involved in, say, developing empathy (a core leadership attribute), is different from the area that is used to understand an intellectual task, such as risk analysis.

A large part of your leadership development should be on creating awareness, developing rapport, influencing and active listening skills.

Developing leadership competencies takes longer, it takes practice and it is largely a personal journey of understanding yourself, your fears and what makes you tick.

Sending employees on a two or three-day training course is largely a 'tick the box' exercise for most organizations (merely an output) that rarely delivers on helping your people transform into great leaders... the real outcome.

Emotional Intelligence involves the circuitry of the brain that runs between the executive centers (prefrontal cortex) and the limbic system, which governs feelings, impulses and drives. Skills based in the limbic areas, research shows, are best learned through motivation, extended practice and feedback. The limbic brain is a much slower learner [than the neocortex used in intellectual learning] particularly when the challenge is to relearn deeply ingrained habits.

This difference matters immensely when trying to improve leadership skills: At their most basic level, those skills come down to habits learned early in life. If those habits are no longer sufficient, or hold a person back, learning takes longer. Re-educating the emotional brain for leadership learning, therefore, requires a different model from what works for the thinking brain: It needs lots of practice and repetition. That's why standard two or three-day leadership training courses don't develop true leadership skills. Leadership cannot really be taught. It can only be learned.

Are you going to continue to be a follower and send your people on the same old "trusted" leadership courses or are you going to be a leader and try something new? Something that will make all the difference!

Do you trust that you have leadership skills in you now or will you rely on a training course to tell you what they are? Are you going to step up and trust yourself... and surprise yourself?

#3: Focusing only on the intellectual competencies...

Management is largely about the 'head'; it's planning and control, systems processes, problem solving, written communications, and so on and it's really important for organizations to have people who excel at these functions. There's no doubt that in order to be competent at any of the above there is a certain level of intelligence (IQ) needed. However, this is management.

Leadership, on the other hand, is all about the heart; it's feelings, it's emotions, it's connectedness, our sense of respect and values. It's about being aware of ourselves and being able to understand others. These competencies are much more intangible and are often referred to as 'soft-skills'... they're called this because they're much harder to grasp. People who exhibit these skills generally have a high Emotional Intelligence (EQ).

However, IQ had little relation to how well they did at work or in the rest of their lives. What made the biggest difference was childhood abilities such as being able to handle frustration, control emotions, and get along with other people.

Measure key soft-skills in all performance reviews - the application and measurement of these will be different for leaders and for staff.

If we are to manage things and lead people we must be able to deal with the whole person but firstly we must be able to deal with ourselves, to manage our thoughts and our emotions. We must learn to 'respond' rather than react. The very word [empathy] seems unbusiness-like, out of place amid the tough realities of the marketplace... Rather, empathy means taking employee's feelings into thoughtful consideration and then making intelligent decisions that work those feelings into the response.

To help develop leadership competencies within an organization is it important Values-Road-Sign to measure the softer skills and adherence to organizational values in a similar manner to the harder skills that normally determine the objectives of a role.

What are your organizational values and what are the behaviors associated with these? How can they be measured and, if an employee is not living up to them, what professional development is available to them?

It is not possible to leave our emotions at the door when we walk into the office. Human beings are emotive creatures and the decisions we make are largely driven by the emotional centers of the brain. Functional Magnetic Resonance Imaging (fMRI) has shown that it is impossible to make a purely intellectual decision without involving those areas that are associated with "gut" responses, empathy and emotional intelligence.

If people do not share a common vision, and do not share a common business reality in which they operate, empowering people will only increase warning-sign organizational stress and the burden of management to maintain coherence and direction. Deepening awareness of personal and corporate ethics and values will enable managers to make decisions and take actions in a consciously principled manner. It is increasingly important that managers model ethics and values to reinforce the organization's standard of conduct.

Leadership is not so much about technique and methods as it is about opening the heart. Leadership is about inspiration-of oneself and of others. Great leadership is about human experiences, not processes. Leadership is not a formula or a program, it is a human activity that comes from the heart and considers the hearts of others. It is an attitude, not a routine.

How can you become more 'emotionally intelligent' in your work environment? What simple steps can you take to draw out the best in your people... and in yourself?

How can you become more in tune with your employees' emotions? How can you help them overcome a challenging time they might be facing to enable to move past it and perform at their best?

#4: Not having a clear development plan for each leader...

For most people who want to develop their career they would look at the qualifications needed to excel in that role. For example, if I was a junior project manager I might focus on getting a PRINCE2 qualification or work towards gaining the points needed to sit the Project Management Institute (PMI) exam and gain accreditation. However, what does a development plan look like for a leader?

Self-development correlates with performance and potential at the manager level though it is not perceived to be important. Being skilled at self-development involves a strong commitment to self-improvement and active effort toward using strengths and making up for weaknesses. Managers tend to be average at this, and we know that it is moderately difficult to develop. However, the simple act of acknowledging the value of self-development can provide managers with more opportunities to put this critical skill into practice.

Because leadership is primarily associated with honing our soft-skills the approach is a little different. Firstly, as mentioned above, developing leadership competencies is largely a personal journey. There are five steps to this process and I would like to concentrate on the first two in this section of the paper.

So how do we develop a deeper awareness of ourselves? Under normal circumstances it's difficult because our subconscious, our ego(s), protect us from anything that may challenge our sense of identity. Change rarely comes from hearing harsh feedback from our boss, it rarely comes from being passed over for promotion. To create lasting change, awareness needs to come from within ourselves and developing such an awareness (and being able to take on feedback) is half the battle to becoming a truly great leader.

Therefore, every leadership development program must involve a heavy component of creating self-awareness in the individual before any lasting change can occur.

"Absolute identity with one's cause is the first and great condition of successful leadership" ~ Woodrow Wilson

Does your leadership development plan include improving on the critical areas of leadership such as self-awareness? Are leadership competencies part of your (and your team's) performance measurements? What do these look like?

How do take on feedback? Do you recognize the different types of feedback you are receiving? Some are subtler than others... Are you aware of your values and do these align with your organization?

5: Leadership strategy is not aligned with business strategy...

The biggest impact on both an organization's current business strategy and on the business futures it needs to create is the way a leader leads his/her team... and the way his/her successor leads their teams.

There needs to be a very clear vision for the organization and every leader should be able to articulate that vision and the strategy proposed to achieve it. Every leader should be able to demonstrate how what they are doing on a day to day basis moves the organization a little closer to achieving its strategy.

Every team member should also know how, by what they do, they contribute to the overall benefit of the team and the organization. They should know that they are more than a cog in the wheel and that what they do is important. It's more than about 'punching the clock' at the beginning and the end of a day; it's about contributing and having a sense of satisfaction in what they do.

And finally, organizations should have a clear picture of what their business strategies should be in 1, 3 or even 15 years out and identify the skills and leadership traits that will be needed a) to get there and b) to maintain momentum and continued growth when it does get there.

Creativity and Innovation Management are two skills that we know correlate with high performance, but these have decreased in both skill and perceived importance since 2003. In order to be competitive, it's time to move out of crisis management and begin to value innovation and the creative process once again. These skills won't be luxuries - they will be critical success factors and possibly a matter of survival for organizations in the next couple of years.